Christmas baking made simple

Exclusive to Howdens Joinery Co.

HOWDENS

JOINERY CO.

MAKING SPACE MORE VALUABLE

Annie Rigg

Christmas baking made simple

The festive season is so much more than just the 'big day'. The anticipation of Christmas is one of my favourite times – it gives you the perfect excuse to bake all sorts of treats you don't normally have throughout the rest of the year. After the big event – from Boxing Day through to New Year, there are still extra family and friends to feed, and maybe parties to organise. So you'll probably want to keep baking!

In this book, I've brought together a wide selection of recipes to make your festive baking quicker and easier – whether you're making cakes, pies, breads, desserts, or decorations and gifts. If you're new to baking, there's plenty here to encourage you to learn. And if you're an experienced hand, you'll find new ideas to inspire your creativity.

Most importantly, I've made all these recipes using Lamona appliances, so I know you'll get brilliant results in your own kitchen. With step-by-step instructions, I've kept everything very simple and straightforward. So you can relax and enjoy your baking, and still have plenty of time to join in the festivities.

Merry Christmas

Annie Rigg

Food writer and stylist

Kitchen featured is Clerkenwell Gloss Grey and Clerkenwell Gloss White

The Christmas Kitchen

Christmas is always a wonderful time to bring friends and family together. The cool and contemporary look of this kitchen contrasts the subtle variation of gloss grey and white with warm oak accents. Personal accessories bringing the magic of Christmas into your home.

A unique island design creates the hub of the kitchen where cooking and entertaining merge into one, while warm integrated LED lighting enhances the welcoming feel of this relaxed, enjoyable space.

The uncluttered design, featuring integrated handles, cleverly conceals all the necessary kitchen storage and accessories – and contains a range of appliances that will help you cook the perfect Christmas dinner.

For further inspiration on how to dress your kitchen for Christmas visit our website at www.howdens.com/advice-inspiration/lamona-cookbook

Perfect baking needs a great oven

When cooking and baking at home, you will want to know you can rely on your oven - to control the temperature and timings accurately, heating evenly for the perfect bake.

With Lamona appliances, exclusive to Howdens Joinery, you have all the reassurance you need. All our appliances are manufactured to the highest standards, to be durable and reliable as well as great value for money. They go through rigorous quality tests, and come with a two-year guarantee plus a five-year guarantee on oven door glass.

Not surprisingly, Lamona is the biggest-selling integrated appliance brand in the UK.

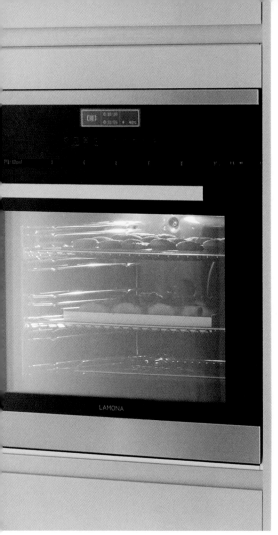

Howdens also offers plenty of choice, so you are sure to find a Lamona oven that fits your kitchen and suits the way you cook – from our touch control built-under double ovens to multi-function ovens. Plus, we offer gas and electric hobs, microwaves, extractors, dishwashers, tumble dryers, fridges and freezers. Everything you need for your ideal kitchen.

All recipes included in this cookbook have been tried and tested using Lamona appliances. Visit www.howdens.com to view our full range of appliances or contact your local depot.

Exclusive to Howdens Joinery Co.

LAMONA APPLIANCE
2 YEAR
GUARANTEE

FESTIVE DECORATIONS

Whether you're making a dramatic centrepiece for the Christmas dinner table or hanging tempting homemade decorations from the tree, you'll find plenty of delicious inspiration here. There are twists on traditional recipes like gingerbread snowmen, and more fun ideas such as edible stained glass biscuits – even some very tasty wreaths!

Star Meringue Wreaths

Pure white meringue is perfect for edible star decorations.
Watch these treats disappear quickly!

Ingredients

300g caster sugar
4 large egg whites
1 pinch salt
Edible silver balls
Ribbon to thread through
the decorations

Equipment

Assorted star-shaped cutters
Piping bag and
star-shaped nozzles
3 baking trays lined with
baking parchment
Electric mixer

1. Pre-heat the oven to 200°C/180°C fan/gas mark 6.

2. Using the cookie cutters as a guide, draw star-shaped outlines on the baking parchment.

3. Tip the sugar into a small roasting tin, and place in the oven for about 5 minutes, until the sugar is hot.

4. Meanwhile, pour the egg whites into the bowl of an electric mixer fitted with a whisk attachment.

5. Whisk the egg whites with a pinch of salt, until they are frothy. Remove the sugar from the oven and immediately turn the heat down to 110°C/90°C fan/gas mark ¼.

6. Add all the hot sugar to the egg whites. Turn the mixer to high speed and continue to whisk for 5 minutes or until the meringue is very stiff, glossy and smooth. If there are still grains of sugar, continue to whisk for another minute.

7. Spoon half the mixture at a time into the piping bag and pipe star meringue shapes onto the parchment-covered baking sheets, using the outlines as a guide. Leave a hole in the middle to thread a ribbon through later.

8. Scatter with edible silver balls and bake in the oven for 45 minutes on the middle shelf or until crisp and dry. Switch the trays around halfway through baking, to ensure they are baked evenly. Turn off the oven and leave the meringues inside to cool down for about 10 minutes.

9. When completely cool, thread ribbon through the shapes and hang straight onto your Christmas tree.

Iced and Spiced Cookies

Christmas baubles you can eat – a great way to make decorating the tree even more fun.

Ingredients

225g unsalted butter, softened
150g icing sugar
1 large egg, beaten
Grated zest of ½ unwaxed lemon
1 tablespoon finely chopped candied ginger
350g plain flour, plus extra for rolling out
1 teaspoon ground ginger
1 teaspoon mixed spice
1 pinch salt
500g royal icing sugar
2 tablespoons lemon juice
Edible silver balls and glitter

Equipment

2 baking sheets lined with baking parchment
Assorted bauble cookie cutters
Disposable piping bags
Ribbon

1. Using a mixer or a large bowl, mix the softened butter and icing sugar until pale, light and fluffy. Gradually add the beaten egg, mixing well until smooth. Add the lemon zest and candied ginger and mix again.

2. Sift the flour, ground ginger, mixed spice and salt into the bowl. Mix until smooth and forms a soft dough.

3. Shape the mixture into a disc and wrap in cling film. Chill in the fridge for a couple of hours or until firm.

4. On a lightly floured work surface, roll out the dough until it is 3mm thick. Using your cutters, stamp out cookies in various sizes and arrange on the prepared baking sheets. With a wooden skewer, push a hole into the top of each cookie – so you can thread string or ribbon through later, to hang the cookies on the tree.

5. Chill the cookies in the fridge for 30 minutes while you pre-heat the oven to 180°C/160°C fan/gas mark 4.

6. Bake the cookies on the middle shelf for 10-12 minutes or until pale golden. Remove from the oven, push the wooden skewer through the holes again if necessary and leave to cool on the baking sheets until firm. Transfer to a wire rack until completely cold.

7. Sift the icing sugar into a bowl. Add enough lemon juice, with a drop of cold water to make a smooth icing that holds a firm ribbon trail. Spoon 4 tablespoons of the icing into a disposable piping bag and use scissors to snip off a tiny nozzle from the tip. Cover the remaining icing in cling film until you need it.

8. Pipe pretty lines and dots across each cookie and decorate with edible silver balls and glitter. Leave until the icing has set firm before threading with ribbon or string and hanging on the tree.

Gingerbread Snowmen

These nostalgic biscuits are fun and easy to prepare and bake – ideal for getting children involved. You can make them in any shape, such as reindeer, Christmas trees, stars or angels.

Ingredients

2 tablespoons golden syrup
1 large egg yolk
200g plain flour,
plus extra for rolling out
½ teaspoon bicarbonate of soda
2 teaspoons ground ginger
1 teaspoon ground cinnamon
½ teaspoon mixed spice
1 pinch salt
100g unsalted butter,
chilled and diced
75g light muscovado sugar
500g royal icing sugar
Red, black and orange food
colouring pastes

Equipment

Rolling pin
Snowman or gingerbread man
biscuit cutters
2 baking sheets lined with
baking parchment
3 disposable piping bags

1. Mix together the golden syrup and egg yolk in a small bowl.

2. Sift the flour, bicarbonate of soda, ginger, cinnamon, mixed spice and salt into a large bowl. Add the chilled, diced butter and rub into the flour using your fingers, trying not to overwork the mixture (you can also do this step in a food processor or mixer fitted with the creamer/paddle attachment).

3. When the mixture resembles fine sand, with no lumps of butter, mix in the light muscovado sugar. Add the golden syrup and egg yolk mixture and mix again until the dough starts to clump together. Use your hands to gently knead the mixture into a smooth ball. Flatten into a disc, wrap in cling film and chill in the fridge for 1 hour.

4. On a lightly floured work surface, roll the dough out to a thickness of 3mm. Using the biscuit cutters, stamp out shapes and arrange on the prepared baking sheets, leaving a little space between each one.

5. Gather any dough scraps together, knead gently into a ball, re-roll and stamp out more biscuits. Chill the biscuits for 15 minutes while you pre-heat the oven to 180°C/160°C fan/gas mark 4.

6. Bake the biscuits on the middle shelf of the oven for 12 minutes, or until they start to brown slightly at the edges.

7. Leave to cool and firm up on the baking sheets for 5 minutes, then place on a wire rack until cold.

8. Sift the royal icing sugar into a bowl. Beating constantly, add cold water, one tablespoon at a time, until the icing holds a firm ribbon trail.

9. Scoop 3 tablespoons of the icing into a disposable piping bag, snip the end to a fine point and pipe an outline of each snowman. Leave to dry for at least 10 minutes.

10. Spoon 3 tablespoons of icing into another bowl. Add red food colouring paste and mix until smooth. Make the black and orange icing in the same way. Cover all the bowls of icing with cling film.

11. Add a drop more water to the remaining white icing. Spoon this carefully into the white outline on each snowman, so the icing floods the space evenly. Use a small palette knife or teaspoon to push the icing into the shapes. Leave to dry for 1 hour.

12. Spoon the red icing into another piping bag, and pipe a scarf onto each snowman. Then pipe black eyes, buttons and a hat, and an orange, carrot-shaped nose. Leave for at least 2 hours, until the icing has completely dried, before you serve or package the biscuits.

Makes 24

Stained Glass Biscuits

Snowflake or star shaped, these biscuits look beautiful hanging at a window or on the Christmas tree, letting the light shine through the 'stained glass'.

Ingredients

225g unsalted butter, softened
150g icing sugar
1 large egg, beaten
1 egg yolk, beaten
1 tablespoon vanilla extract
350g plain flour,
plus extra for rolling out
1 teaspoon ground ginger
1 teaspoon ground cinnamon
1 pinch salt
200g assorted flavoured and
coloured boiled sweets

Equipment

Snowflake or star-shaped cutters
in assorted sizes
2 baking sheets lined with
baking parchment
Freezer bags
Electric mixer or hand whisk
Rolling pin

1. Using an electric mixer with a paddle attachment or an electric hand whisk, mix the softened butter and icing sugar together until pale and light. Add the whole egg, egg yolk and vanilla extract, and mix again until thoroughly combined.

2. Sift the plain flour with the ginger, cinnamon and salt, into to the bowl and mix again until smooth.

3. Gather the dough into a ball, flatten into a disc and wrap in cling film. Chill in the fridge for a couple of hours or until firm.

4. Meanwhile, divide the boiled sweets into separate colours and place each colour in a double thickness of freezer bags and crush into small pieces using a rolling pin.

5. Pre-heat the oven to 180°C/160°C fan/gas mark 4.

6. On a lightly floured work surface, roll out the dough until it is 3mm thick. Using the biscuit cutters, stamp out shapes in assorted sizes and arrange on the prepared baking sheets. Stamp out the middle of each biscuit leaving a neat hole in the middle. Carefully fill each hole with one colour of the crushed boiled sweets, filling them just shallower than the depth of the biscuits.

7. Bake in batches on the middle shelf of the oven for 12 minutes, until the biscuits are pale golden and the boiled sweets have melted and completely filled the holes.

8. Gather any dough scraps into a neat ball, re-roll and shape more biscuits as before.

9. Cool the biscuits on the trays until they have hardened. When cool, thread string or ribbon through the holes.

Cupcake Tree

Makes about 48
mini muffin cupcakes,
2 cupcake trees

10 mins preparation
12 mins cooking
20 mins decorating

A spectacular centrepiece for a Christmas party, this tree is far easier to make than it looks – and tastes even better!

Ingredients

175g unsalted butter, at
room temperature
175g caster sugar
3 large eggs, lightly beaten
1 tablespoon vanilla extract
200g plain flour
2 teaspoons baking powder
3 teaspoons milk, at
room temperature

For the buttercream

250g unsalted butter,
at room temperature
500g icing sugar, sifted
2 teaspoons vanilla extract
2 tablespoons milk,
at room temperature
Green food colouring paste
Edible silver glitter
Edible star and
snowflake decorations
Green hundreds and thousands
or sugar strands
Foil-wrapped sweets for decoration

Equipment

24-hole mini muffin baking tray
48 green mini muffin paper chase
Electric mixer
14cm polystyrene cone
(from arts and crafts shops)
Cocktail sticks
Piping bag and star-shaped nozzle
Shimmer or glitter food
colour spray (optional)

1. Pre-heat the oven to 170°C/150°C fan/gas mark 3 and line the mini muffin baking tray with 24 of the paper cases.

2. Mix 175g butter with the caster sugar until really pale and light – it is easiest to use an electric mixer.

3. Gradually add the beaten eggs and vanilla, mixing well between each addition. Sift the flour and baking powder into the bowl, add the milk and mix again until smooth.

4. Divide the cake mix into two. Use one half to fill the first 24 paper cases, each with about 1 rounded teaspoon of mix. Bake on the middle shelf for 11 minutes until well-risen and pale golden. Check the cakes are cooked by inserting a wooden skewer into the middle – it should come out clean.

5. Transfer the cakes to a cooling rack. Working quickly, line the muffin tray with 24 more cases. Fill with the remaining cake mix and bake as before.

6. To make the buttercream, place the softened butter in the bowl of an electric mixer and beat for 2 minutes until pale and soft. Sift the icing sugar into the bowl and roughly fold in using a rubber spatula. Add the vanilla and milk and beat again until smooth. Add the food colouring paste and mix until thoroughly combined.

7. Spoon the buttercream into the piping bag, fitted with a star nozzle. Ensuring the cakes are cold, pipe rosettes over the top of each cake. Decorate with silver balls, glitter, edible decorations, and hundreds and thousands.

8. Push a cocktail stick into the bottom of each cake and use the sticks to arrange the cakes around the polystyrene cone – starting at the bottom and working to the top to create a Christmas tree effect. You can fill any gaps with foil-wrapped sweets.

9. Place the cone on a cake stand and tie a festive ribbon around the base, add shimmer or glitter food colour spray if required.

Chef's note... Alternative cone sizes are available to buy and there are no restrictions on the size of your cupcake tree, just ensure the ingredients are adapted where necessary.

FESTIVE DESSERTS

Christmas is a time when we're all allowed to indulge a little. Here I've taken fruity, spicy, festive flavours and created some new takes on classic desserts like gingery plum pudding and pavlova with baked plum compote. If you can't enjoy it now, when can you?

Serves 6-8

30 mins preparation
40 mins cooking

Pear, Chocolate, Apricot and Almond Strudel

Ingredients

4 conference pears
100g unsalted butter
2 tablespoons caster sugar
1 teaspoon vanilla bean paste
1 teaspoon ground cinnamon
125g dried apricots, chopped
50g Amaretti biscuits
100g marzipan
50g dark chocolate
8 sheets filo pastry

Equipment

Large baking tray lined with baking parchment
Frying pan

If you like the combination of pear and chocolate, you will love this almondy strudel – a truly satisfying dessert!

1. Peel, quarter and core the pears, then cut into large chunks.

2. Melt 25g of the unsalted butter in a frying pan. Add the pears, 1 tablespoon of caster sugar, and the vanilla and cinnamon. Cook over a medium heat until the pears start to soften at the edges and caramelise.

3. Roughly chop the apricots and add to the pan. Stir well, then remove from the heat and leave to cool.

4. Meanwhile, crush the Amaretti biscuits into small pieces, finely dice the marzipan and finely chop the chocolate.

5. Melt the remaining butter in either a small pan or the microwave.

6. Pre-heat the oven to 190°C/170°C fan/gas mark 5.

7. Lay one sheet of filo pastry on the work surface, with the long side closest to you and brush all over with melted butter. Lay another pastry sheet on top and brush with more butter. Repeat this layering of pastry and butter until you have 8 layers.

8. Scatter the crushed Amaretti pieces over the top of the pastry, leaving a 2cm border around the edge. Spoon the pears and apricots over the Amaretti, then top with the marzipan and chopped chocolate.

9. Brush the edges with butter and fold the two short sides of the pastry over the filling to prevent any bits escaping. Brush the edges again with butter and roll the pastry up and over the filling like a Swiss roll. Try to keep the roll as tight as possible, and the sides neatly tucked in.

10. Lift the strudel carefully onto the lined baking tray. Brush with more butter across the top, sprinkle with the remaining sugar and bake on the middle shelf of the oven for 40 minutes, or until the pastry is crisp and golden.

11. Serve warm or at room temperature, cut into thick slices and with lashings of rich double cream.

Serves 8

25 mins preparation
1 hour cooking

Cranberry Topped Cheesecake

A classic layer cheesecake recipe gets the festive treatment with this luscious cranberry and Cointreau topping.

Ingredients

50g unsalted butter,
plus a little extra for greasing
150g digestive or ginger
snap biscuits
600g full-fat cream cheese
3 large eggs
300ml soured cream
175g caster sugar
1 tablespoon cornflour
1 teaspoon vanilla bean paste
Juice and grated zest of 1
unwaxed lemon
100g Greek-style yoghurt

For the topping
350g cranberries
175g caster sugar
1 teaspoon vanilla bean paste
2 tablespoons Cointreau or
Grand Marnier
Juice of ½ orange
1-2 teaspoons cornflour

Equipment
20cm side-opening cake tin,
lined with baking parchment
Food processor
Baking sheet

1. Pre-heat the oven to 170°C/150°C fan/gas mark 3. Butter the base of the tin and line with a disc of buttered baking parchment.

2. Crush the biscuits in a food processor or put them in a freezer bag and bash with a rolling pin. Place in a bowl.

3. Melt the butter and mix into the biscuit crumbs. Place in the prepared tin and press into an even layer over the base. Bake on the middle shelf of the oven for 5 minutes.

4. In a bowl, combine the cream cheese, eggs, half of the soured cream, 125g of caster sugar and the tablespoon of cornflour. Blitz until smooth, then add the vanilla, lemon juice and zest and blitz again.

5. Carefully pour the mixture into the tin. Place on a baking sheet and bake on the middle shelf of the oven for 35 minutes, or until just set.

6. Remove from the oven and leave to rest for 10 minutes – but keep the oven on.

7. Meanwhile, beat together the remaining soured cream and 50g of caster sugar with the Greek-style yoghurt. Carefully spoon this mixture on top of the cheesecake and return to the oven for a further 15 minutes, or until set but not coloured.

8. Remove the cheesecake from the oven and leave to cool completely before chilling in the fridge.

9. To prepare the topping, place half of the cranberries in a pan with the sugar, vanilla and Cointreau or Grand Marnier. Cook over a medium heat, until the cranberries burst and start to release their juice. Add the remaining cranberries and cook for a moment longer to soften them. Mix the orange juice and cornflour together in a small bowl. Add to the cranberry mixture, stirring constantly as it slightly thickens.

10. Remove from the heat, pour into a bowl and leave until cold.

11. Carefully remove the cheesecake from the tin and place on a serving plate. Top with the cranberry compote.

Pavlova with Baked Plum Compote

A fruit-topped pavlova always creates a sense of occasion. Here, port-baked plums add a distinct seasonal touch.

Ingredients

6 large egg whites
325g caster sugar
1 pinch salt
3 teaspoons cornflour
1 teaspoon vanilla bean paste
1 teaspoon cider vinegar or white wine vinegar
50g flaked almonds

For the plum compote

1.5kg red plums
2-3 tablespoons clear honey
150ml port or Marsala
3 star anise

To serve

500ml double cream
50g icing sugar
1 teaspoon vanilla bean paste

Equipment

Electric mixer
2 baking sheets
Baking parchment

1. Pre-heat the oven to 170°C/150°C fan/gas mark 3.

2. Place the egg whites in the bowl of an electric mixer with a whisk attachment. Add the caster sugar and salt and whisk on high speed for 10 minutes, or until the mixture is thick and glossy white and all the sugar is mixed in. You should not be able to see or taste any grains of sugar. If you do, mix for another minute and check again. Add the cornflour, vanilla and vinegar, and whisk again thoroughly.

3. Take 2 large sheets of baking parchment and draw a 20cm circle in the middle of each one, using a cake tin as a guide. Lay the parchment on the baking sheets.

4. Divide the meringue mix evenly between the two circles. Use a palette knife to spread into discs. Around the sides of each meringue, drag the tip of the palette knife upwards at regular intervals to make decorative sides to the pavlova. Scatter with flaked almonds and slide the meringues into the oven. Immediately reduce the temperature to 100°C/80°C fan/gas mark ¼ and bake for 1 hour 15 minutes, swapping the trays around halfway through to ensure the meringues bake evenly.

5. Turn off the oven and leave the meringues inside to cool down for 1 hour (or even better left overnight), then leave the door ajar until the meringues are completely cold.

6. When cool, pre-heat the oven to 180°C/160°C fan/gas mark 4.

7. Wash the plums, cut in half and remove the stones. Lay in a single layer, cut side up, in a large ovenproof dish. Drizzle the honey over the plums, add the port (or Marsala) and star anise, and bake on the middle shelf of the oven for 35 minutes or until tender.

8. Using a slotted spoon, transfer three quarters of the plums to a shallow serving dish and the rest into a nylon sieve. Pour the cooking liquid into a small saucepan, reduce by half and remove from the heat. Push the plums through the sieve, then add the resulting purée to the reduced liquid. Pour over the plums in the serving dish and set aside until cold.

9. In a clean electric mixer bowl, whip the cream with the icing sugar and vanilla until it holds soft peaks.

10. Place one of the meringues on the serving plate and spread with half of the cream. Top with one third of the plum compote. Repeat this layering with the second meringue, remaining cream and another third of the plums. Serve immediately with the remaining plums alongside.

Serves 6

30 mins preparation
3 hours cooking

Gingery Plum Pudding

Try this twist on the traditional Christmas pudding – it could become a new family favourite!

Ingredients

100g unsalted butter,
at room temperature,
plus a little extra for greasing
3 tablespoons golden syrup,
plus a little extra for serving
275g mixed raisins, sultanas,
currants and dried cranberries
100g soft prunes, chopped
50g crystallised stem ginger,
finely chopped
100ml ginger wine
Finely grated zest and juice
of 1 orange
100g almonds, chopped
1 small Bramley apple, peeled,
cored and coarsely grated
100g dark muscovado sugar
2 large eggs, lightly beaten
125g self-raising flour
½ teaspoon baking powder
1 teaspoon ground ginger
1 teaspoon mixed spice

To serve

Thick cream, brandy butter
or custard

Equipment

1.5 litre pudding basin or bowl
Baking parchment

1. Butter the inside of the pudding basin and spoon the golden syrup into the base.

2. Put all the dried fruit in a large pan. Add the chopped ginger, ginger wine, orange zest and juice. Cook on a low heat for 10 minutes or until most of the liquid has been absorbed. Remove from the heat and when cool, add the almonds and apple, and mix well.

3. Beat together the butter and sugar until creamy. Gradually beat in the eggs, mixing well between each addition. Sift the flour, baking powder, ground ginger and mixed spice into the bowl and fold in using a large metal spoon. Stir in the dried fruit mixture, with any unabsorbed liquid.

4. Spoon the mixture into the pudding basin and level. Cover with a sheet of baking parchment and then a sheet of foil. Make a pleat in the middle to allow the pudding to expand, then tie the cover securely with string under the rim of the bowl, trimming off any excess.

5. Place the pudding in a large saucepan and fill with boiling water to reach two thirds up the side of the pudding bowl. Cover with a lid and simmer on a low heat for 3 hours, checking the water level halfway through the cooking time. Add more boiling water if needed.

6. Remove the pudding from the pan. Let it rest for 5 minutes, then turn out onto a warm serving dish. Gently warm a little extra golden syrup and spoon over the pudding before serving with cream, clementine and brandy butter or cinnamon custard (see page 72 for accompaniment recipes).

Malted Custard Tart with Boozy Raisins

Serves 6
1 hour preparation
45 mins cooking

A rich egg custard tart, with a warming glow of Bourbon-soaked raisins and a grating of chocolate. When else, but at Christmas?

Ingredients

For the boozy raisins
100g raisins
4 tablespoons Bourbon or Marsala
1 small cinnamon stick

For the pastry
200g plain flour,
plus extra for rolling out
40g icing sugar
1 good pinch salt
1 teaspoon mixed spice
125g unsalted butter,
chilled and diced
1 large egg yolk
2 tablespoons ice cold water
2 teaspoons lemon juice or
cider vinegar

For the custard
5 large egg yolks
40g light muscovado sugar
20g caster sugar
1 teaspoon vanilla bean paste
2 tablespoons barley malt extract
1 pinch sea salt flakes
250ml double cream
125ml whole milk
1 good grating of nutmeg
50g dark chocolate,
coarsely grated

Equipment
Food processor
22cm tart tin, 3-4cm deep

1. Place the raisins in a small saucepan with the Bourbon (or Marsala) and cinnamon stick. Warm gently over a low heat without boiling. Stir well and set aside for 2 hours. Better still, leave overnight so the raisins soak up all the alcohol.

2. Meanwhile, make the pastry. Place the plain flour, icing sugar, salt and mixed spice in a food processor bowl. Add the butter, and pulse to mix until there are no visible pieces of butter and the mixture resembles breadcrumbs. Add the egg yolk, water and lemon juice or vinegar. Mix again to form a dough.

3. Using your hands, shape the dough into a ball, then flatten into a disc. Cover with cling film and chill in the fridge for an hour until firm.

4. On a lightly floured work surface, roll out the pastry into a disc, about 2mm thick. Use this to line the tart tin, working carefully. Trim off any excess pastry, prick the base and chill for 20 minutes while you pre-heat the oven to 180°C/160°C fan/gas mark 4.

5. Line the tin with scrunched up foil or baking parchment, and fill with baking beans or rice. Bake on the middle shelf of the oven for around 18 minutes, or until crisp and slightly golden. Remove the foil or parchment and baking beans, then cook the pastry for another 2 minutes to dry out the base.

6. To prepare the custard, turn the oven down to 170°C/150°C fan/gas mark 3. Place the egg yolks in a mixing bowl, add both the sugars and whisk to combine. Add the vanilla, malt extract and sea salt flakes. Whisk again gently until smooth.

7. In a small pan, heat the cream and milk until the surface shimmers, just below boiling. Pour onto the egg and sugar mixture, whisking constantly until thoroughly combined. Try not to let too much air into the custard. Strain through a fine sieve into a jug, then leave to cool to room temperature.

8. Using a slotted spoon, scoop the raisins into the pastry case and place the tin on a baking tray. Pour the custard on top, being careful not to spill any over the edges of the pastry. Grate nutmeg over the top and bake for 20-25 minutes until the custard has just set.

9. Leave to cool in the tin for 30 minutes, then transfer from the tin to a wire rack to cool further. Serve at room temperature, scattered with grated chocolate.

FESTIVE BREADS

Sweet or savoury, loaves, rolls or 'tear and share' bread is so versatile. Serve with a meal or make it star of the show. There's something for any part of the festive season.

Serves 6-8

40 mins preparation
plus 2 hours proving time
40 mins cooking

Cinnamon and Pecan Tear and Share Bread

With a satisfyingly soft texture and a nutty crunch, this sweet treat is perfect for festive family get-togethers.

Ingredients

125ml whole milk
2 teaspoons dried active yeast
1 teaspoon maple syrup
250g strong white flour,
plus extra for kneading
100g white spelt flour
40g caster sugar,
plus extra for sprinkling on top
½ teaspoon salt
1 large egg, beaten
1 large egg yolk, lightly beaten
60g unsalted butter,
at room temperature

For the filling

75g unsalted butter,
at room temperature
75g soft light brown sugar
2 teaspoons cinnamon
100g pecan nuts

Equipment

Loaf tin with a 23cm x 9cm base
and 8cm in depth, lined with
baking parchment
Small pan
Electric mixer with dough hook
Baking sheet
Jug

1. Warm the milk in a small pan, or in the microwave. Add the yeast and maple syrup and whisk to combine. Set aside in a warm place for 5-10 minutes until the yeast has created a thick foam on top.

2. Tip the flours into the bowl of an electric mixer with a dough hook. Add the caster sugar and salt, and mix well. Make a well in the middle, and pour in the milk and yeast mixture. Add the beaten egg, egg yolk and butter. Mix thoroughly until combined. Turn the dough out onto a lightly floured work surface and knead for about 5 minutes until the dough is smooth and elastic.

3. Shape the dough into a ball, place in a clean bowl and cover with cling film. Leave in a warming drawer or draught-free place for about 1½ hours or until the dough has doubled in size.

4. While the dough is proving, prepare the cinnamon butter filling. Cream together the butter, sugar and cinnamon until soft and smooth.

5. Chop the pecans and set aside.

6. Turn the dough back onto the floured work surface and knead for 30 seconds to knock out any air. Roll the dough into a rectangle, roughly 40cm x 20cm, with the long edge closest to you.

7. Spread the cinnamon butter evenly over the dough and scatter with the chopped pecans. Cut the dough into 3 horizontally, and then in half vertically to make 6 smaller rectangles. Cut each rectangle into 3, giving you 18 small rectangles.

8. Stack the dough pieces into piles of 3 and then arrange them upright in the prepared loaf tin so they look like slices. Cover loosely with cling film and leave for 45 minutes until risen to just over the top of the tin.

9. Pre-heat the oven to 190°C/170°C fan/gas mark 5.

10. Remove the cling film and sprinkle the top of the loaf with extra caster sugar. Place on a baking sheet on the middle shelf of the oven for about 30 minutes or until golden brown and well risen.

11. Leave the loaf to cool in the tin for 40 minutes, then turn out onto a wire rack.

Chef's note... This tear and share loaf is best served on the day you make it.

Stollen Spirals

Based on the classic German fruit bread, these spirals are rich, sticky and full of Christmas flavour.

Ingredients

100g mixed raisins, sultanas and currants
25g dried cranberries
40g chopped candied peel
50g glacé cherries, quartered
Finely grated zest and juice of 1 orange
2 tablespoons brandy or dark rum
125ml whole milk
7g dried active yeast
25g caster sugar
275g strong white bread flour, plus extra for rolling out
½ teaspoon mixed spice
¼ teaspoon ground cinnamon
½ teaspoon salt
50g unsalted butter, softened
1 medium egg, lightly beaten
1 teaspoon vanilla extract or vanilla bean paste
25g whole almonds, roughly chopped
25g pistachios, roughly chopped
175g marzipan, diced
Icing sugar for dusting

Equipment

30cm x 20cm x 5cm baking tin, lined with baking parchment
Electric mixer with dough hook
Small pan
Rolling pin

1. Tip all the dried fruit into a small pan. Add the grated orange zest, juice and brandy or rum, and heat to just below boiling point. Take off the heat and leave the fruit to cool for up to 2 hours, until it absorbs all the liquid.

2. Heat the milk to lukewarm, then pour into a jug. Add the yeast and a teaspoon of caster sugar. Whisk well to combine. Set aside for 5-10 minutes, until the yeast has formed a thick, foamy crust.

3. In a bowl, add the flour, the rest of the caster sugar, mixed spice, cardamom and salt. Make a well in the middle and add the softened butter, egg, vanilla and yeasty milk. Mix until combined using the dough hook, then continue to mix for about 5 minutes until the dough is smooth and elastic. Shape the dough into a ball, place in a large bowl, cover with cling film and leave in a warming drawer or a draught-free spot until doubled in size.

4. Turn the dough out onto a lightly floured work surface, and knead lightly for 30 seconds. Gently roll out the dough into a rectangle, roughly 50cm x 30cm, with the long side nearest to you. Scatter the plump dried fruit, chopped almonds and pistachios, and diced marzipan evenly over the top of the dough.

5. Roll the dough carefully into a tight spiral, starting from the long edge nearest to you and neatly encasing the filling.

6. When you have a neat log, with the seal underneath, cut it into 12 even-sized pieces. Arrange these, laid flat, in the prepared tin. Cover loosely with cling film, and leave to rise for 45 minutes.

7. Pre-heat the oven to 180°C/160°C fan/gas mark 4.

8. Remove the cling film, and bake the stollen spirals on the middle shelf of the oven for about 25 minutes, or until golden brown.

9. Leave to cool completely before dusting with icing sugar to serve.

Rye and Mixed Seed Bread

30 mins preparation
including cooling time
plus 2 hours proving time
1 hour cooking

Make this bread the day before you plan to serve it, so the flavours have time to mellow. It's delicious with smoked salmon, cream cheese and pickles.

Ingredients

350g wholemeal rye flour
150g wholemeal spelt flour
50g rye flakes or spelt flakes
50g medium oatmeal
400ml boiling water
10g dried active yeast
50g black treacle, plus 1 teaspoon
1 rounded teaspoon caraway seeds
75g mixed seeds (pumpkin, linseed, sunflower and sesame), plus extra for sprinkling
1 tablespoon olive oil
1 teaspoon salt
2 teaspoons milk

Equipment

Loaf tin with a 23cm x 9cm base and 8cm in depth, greased with butter and lined with baking parchment

1. Place the flours in a large mixing bowl with the rye or spelt flakes and oatmeal. Pour in 400ml boiling water and mix until just combined. Set aside for 30 minutes to cool down.

2. Pour 50ml warm water into a small bowl, then add the yeast and mix well to combine. Set aside for 5-10 minutes until foam appears on top of the mixture.

3. Pour the yeast mixture, 50g of treacle, caraway seeds, mixed seeds, olive oil and salt into the flour mixture. Mix well until thoroughly combined. Cover the bowl loosely with cling film and set aside for 1 hour to allow the dough to rise to the top of the tin.

4. Knead for 1 minute to knock back the dough to remove the air, then place in the prepared loaf tin. Press it level with either a damp hand or back of a spoon. Cover loosely with oiled cling film and keep in a warming drawer or draught-free place for 1-1½ hours, or until the dough rises just above the edge of the tin. It will not rise as much as conventional bread.

5. Pre-heat the oven to 200°C/180°C fan/gas mark 6.

6. Mix the milk with a teaspoon of treacle and gently brush over the top of the loaf. Sprinkle with the extra seeds and bake on the middle shelf of the oven for 15 minutes. Reduce the heat to 190°C/170°C fan/gas mark 5 and cook for a further 45 minutes until the loaf sounds hollow when tapped.

7. Leave to cool in the tin for 5 minutes, then turn out onto a wire rack. When completely cold, wrap in foil and keep for 24 hours before serving.

Makes 12 rolls

20 mins preparation
plus 1 hour 30 mins
proving time
25 mins cooking

Sage and Onion Bread Rolls

Offer your guests something different with these tasty rolls. Perfect with a hearty bowl of soup, or any festive starter.

Ingredients

1 large onion
1 tablespoon olive oil
Salt and freshly ground
black pepper
1 tablespoon finely chopped sage
350g strong white flour,
plus extra for rolling out
175g plain flour
7g fast-action/easy-bake yeast
250ml whole milk,
plus 1 tablespoon for brushing
1 tablespoon malt extract
1 large egg, lightly beaten
50g unsalted butter,
at room temperature
1-2 tablespoons poppy seeds

Equipment

2 baking sheets lined with
baking parchment
Electric mixer with dough hook
Frying pan

1. Peel and slice the onion. In a frying pan, heat the olive oil and sliced onion, and season with salt and black pepper. Cook over a low-medium heat until soft and starting to caramelise. Remove from the heat, add the chopped sage and leave to cool.

2. Tip the flours into a bowl and add the yeast and ½ teaspoon of salt, using an electric mixer with a dough hook to combine.

3. In a small pan, heat the milk, but do not let it boil. Add the malt extract and mix to combine, then pour into the mixer bowl along with the beaten egg and butter. Mix until combined, then continue to knead until the dough is smooth and elastic.

4. Shape the dough into a ball and place back in the bowl. Cover loosely with cling film or a clean, damp tea towel and leave in a warming drawer or a draught-free place for 45 minutes to 1 hour until doubled in size.

5. Turn the dough out onto a lightly floured work surface. Flatten slightly and add the sage and onion. Knead for a minute to knock back any air and to mix in the onions and sage.

6. Divide the dough into 12 even pieces.

7. Shape into neat balls with the seal on the underside and arrange on parchment-lined baking sheets. Cover loosely with oiled cling film and leave to prove in a warming drawer or draught-free place for 45 minutes, until well risen and puffy.

8. Pre-heat the oven to 190°C/170°C fan/gas mark 5.

9. Carefully brush the top of each roll with milk and sprinkle with poppy seeds. Use a sharp knife to cut a cross in the top of each roll. Bake on the middle shelf of the oven for about 20-25 minutes until well-risen and golden brown. The rolls should sound hollow when you tap them on the underside.

Chef's note... Use an electric mixer rather than your hands to mix the dough, as it may be slightly sticky.

Serves 6-8

15 mins preparation
40 mins cooking

Carrot and Courgette Loaf

This wheat-free loaf is delicious simply spread with butter or a mustard dip (see page 70) – it also goes perfectly with soup, cold meats or festive leftovers.

Ingredients

250g spelt flour
2 teaspoons baking powder
½ teaspoon paprika
½ teaspoon garlic granules
1 pinch salt
Freshly ground black pepper
3 spring onions
100g coarsely grated carrot
75g coarsely grated courgette
100g grated Gruyère or
mature Cheddar
2 teaspoons kalonji seeds
3 large eggs, lightly beaten
100g virgin olive oil

Equipment

Loaf tin with a 23cm x 9cm base
and 8cm in depth, greased
with butter and lined with
baking parchment

1. Pre-heat the oven to 190°C/170°C fan/gas mark 5.

2. Sift the flour, baking powder, paprika and garlic granules into a large bowl, and season well with salt and black pepper.

3. Trim and finely chop the spring onions.

4. Make a well in the middle of the dry ingredients. Add the spring onions, carrot, courgette, and all but 1 tablespoon of grated cheese. Add 1 teaspoon of the kalonji seeds along with the beaten eggs and olive oil. Mix well.

5. Spoon the batter into the prepared loaf tin. The batter will be quite stiff, so you may need to use the back of a spoon to level the top of the loaf. Sprinkle with the remaining cheese and kalonji seeds. Bake on the middle shelf of the oven for 40 minutes until risen and golden brown. Check the batter is cooked by inserting a skewer into the middle – it should come out clean.

6. Leave to cool in the tin for 10 minutes, then turn out onto a wire rack.

7. Serve warm or at room temperature. Can also be frozen or will keep for 2-3 days if well wrapped in foil.

Chef's note... The mix for this bread does not form a dough – so no kneading required!

FAMILY BAKING

Christmas is all about families getting together and sharing delicious food, so it's the perfect time to try out these cake and pie recipes - and, of course, to treat the kids. I've included a speedy shortcut to an irresistible Christmas cake, and extra-luxurious mince pies. Plus a mouth-watering layer cake and a wonderful gluten-free orange-chocolate creation. Sausage rolls are on the menu too, but not as you've had them before!

**30 mins preparation
plus 1 hour chilling
20-25 mins cooking**

Mincemeat Crumble Pies

The cream cheese pastry in this recipe takes mince pies to another level – especially when paired with my nutty crumble topping.

Ingredients

For the pastry

150g plain flour,
plus extra for rolling out
½ teaspoon baking powder
25g caster sugar
1 pinch salt
75g unsalted butter,
chilled and diced
75g cream cheese
50g ground almonds
1 medium egg yolk
1 tablespoon milk

For the crumble topping

75g light soft brown sugar
75g plain flour
1 teaspoon ground cinnamon
50g finely chopped almonds
40g unsalted butter, melted
400g luxury mincemeat
Icing sugar for dusting

Equipment

Food processor
2 x 12-hole bun trays
8-9cm fluted pastry cutter
Rolling pin

1. To make the pastry, place the flour, baking powder, sugar and salt in the food processor bowl. Add the butter, and use the pulse button to rub it into the dry ingredients, until the mixture resembles fine sand.

2. Add the cream cheese, ground almonds, egg yolk and milk, and mix again until a dough starts to form. Place in a mixing bowl and use your hands to make a neat ball – but do not overwork it. Flatten into a disc, cover with cling film and leave in the fridge for 1 hour.

3. Lightly dust the work surface with plain flour. Divide the dough in two and roll out one half until it is around 2mm thick. Using the pastry cutter, stamp out as many discs from the dough as you can. Use them to line the bun trays, pressing gently with your fingers.

4. Gather the dough scraps together and set aside. Roll out the second half of the dough and stamp out more pastry discs, continuing to line the bun trays. Gather all the dough scraps together and press gently into a ball. Roll this out and stamp out more discs – you should aim for 24 pastry cases in total.

5. Chill the pastry in the fridge for 30 minutes while you pre-heat the oven to 180°C/160°C fan/gas mark 4 and make the crumble topping. To do this, place the sugar, flour, cinnamon and almonds in a bowl, then add the melted butter and use your fingers to combine.

6. Spoon the mincemeat into each pastry case and top with a little of the crumble mixture. Bake on the middle shelf of the oven for about 20 minutes or until golden brown. Leave to cool in the bun trays for 10 minutes, then remove carefully and transfer to a wire rack to cool completely. Serve the pies warm and dust with a little icing sugar.

Quick Christmas Cake

Save precious preparation time with this quick Christmas cake recipe. All the festive flavours of a traditional cake, but made in a fraction of the time.

Ingredients

175g unsalted butter,
at room temperature
75g glacé cherries,
rinsed and halved
50g candied peel
75g dried cranberries
450g mixed dried fruit
(sultanas, raisins, currants)
Finely grated zest and juice
of ½ lemon
Finely grated zest and juice
of 1 orange
4 tablespoons brandy
50g blanched almonds,
roughly chopped
100g light soft brown sugar
50g golden syrup
50g black treacle
3 large eggs, lightly beaten
225g strong white bread flour
50g ground almonds
1 teaspoon baking powder
2 teaspoons mixed spice
1 pinch salt
2 tablespoons milk

To decorate

3 tablespoons apricot jam
Mixture of dried apricots,
pecans, pistachios,
glacé cherries and almonds

Equipment

20cm deep diameter cake tin
Baking parchment
Electric mixer
Large saucepan

1. Butter the inside of the tin and line the base and sides with a double thickness of buttered baking parchment.

2. Place all the candied and dried fruit in a large saucepan. Add the lemon and orange zest and juice. Add the brandy, mix well, and warm over a low heat – do not let it boil. Remove from the heat and set aside to cool for 1 hour, stirring occasionally. This lets the fruit become plump with all the juice and brandy. Once cooled, add the chopped almonds to the fruit.

3. Pre-heat the oven to 150°C/130°C fan/gas mark 2.

4. Using an electric mixer, combine the softened butter and brown sugar until pale and light. Add the golden syrup and treacle. Mix again.

5. Gradually add the beaten eggs, mixing well between each addition.

6. Sift the flour, ground almonds, baking powder, mixed spice and salt into the bowl. Add the milk and mix again thoroughly.

7. Scoop the cake mixture into the prepared tin. Spread level with the back of a spoon and bake just below the middle shelf for 2 hours or until a skewer inserted into the middle comes out clean. If the cake seems to be browning too quickly, cover loosely with foil.

8. Leave to cool in the tin for 30 minutes, then transfer to a wire rack to cool down completely.

9. Wrap in foil and leave overnight before decorating.

10. Warm and sieve the apricot jam and brush over the top of the cake. Arrange the fruit and nuts attractively on top, brush with more warmed apricot jam and leave until it is set before serving.

Gluten-Free Orange and Almond Cake

Orange and chocolate is a marriage made in heaven. Here, there is just a subtle hint of dark chocolate, plus the delicious complexity of cinnamon and cardamom.

Ingredients

200g unsalted butter,
at room temperature,
125g gluten-free plain flour,
plus a little extra for dusting
2 clementines
50g dark chocolate
200g caster sugar
3 large eggs, lightly beaten
2 teaspoons baking powder
½ teaspoon ground cinnamon
1 pinch salt
200g ground almonds

For the syrup

2 clementines (or 1 orange)
Juice of ½ lemon
125g caster sugar
1 cinnamon stick
3 cardamom pods, bruised

Equipment

Bundt or kugelhopf tin,
preferably non-stick
Food processor
Electric mixer

1. Melt a little butter and brush it thoroughly around the inside of the baking tin. Lightly dust the tin with a little gluten-free flour. Tap on the work surface to loosen any excess flour and set aside.

2. Wash the clementines and place whole in a small saucepan. Cover with water and set the pan over a medium heat. Bring to the boil, reduce to a simmer and cook for 45 minutes to 1 hour, or until soft. Drain and leave to cool.

3. Pre-heat the oven to 190°C/170°C fan/gas mark 5.

4. Cut the cooked clementines into quarters and remove the pithy core and any pips. Place the fruit (including the skin) in a food processor. Blend until pulpy and almost smooth, then set aside. Coarsely grate the dark chocolate.

5. Combine the butter and caster sugar in an electric mixer until pale and light. Gradually add the beaten eggs, mixing well between each addition.

6. Add the puréed clementines and mix again – at this stage, the mixture may look curdled, but do not worry. Sift the flour, baking powder, cinnamon and salt into the bowl. Add the ground almonds and grated chocolate, and mix again thoroughly.

7. Spoon the mixture into the prepared tin, spread level and bake on the middle shelf of the oven for 35-40 minutes, or until golden and risen. Check the cake is cooked by inserting a wooden skewer into the middle – it should come out with a moist crumb attached.

8. Leave the cake to rest in the tin for 5 minutes, then carefully turn out onto a wire rack to cool.

9. To make the syrup, remove the peel from the clementines (or orange) in strips, using a vegetable peeler. Slice the peel into fine shreds and soften in boiling water for 1 minute.

10. Squeeze the juice from the clementines (or orange) and pour into a small pan with the lemon juice. Add the caster sugar, cinnamon stick, cardamom pods and 2 tablespoons of water. Bring to the boil, then simmer until reduced by half and slightly thickened to a pourable syrup. Remove the cinnamon stick and cardamom pods, add the peel and simmer for a further 30 seconds. Leave to cool slightly.

11. Carefully and slowly spoon the syrup and peel over the cake. Serve with any extra syrup and peel alongside.

Spiced Maple Syrup and Pecan Cake

This luxurious layer cake with a meringue frosting keeps well for a couple of days in an airtight container – so you can prepare ahead.

Ingredients

175g unsalted butter, softened
100g pecan nuts
275g plain flour
2 teaspoons baking powder
1 teaspoon bicarbonate of soda
1 teaspoon ground cinnamon
1 good grating of nutmeg
1 pinch salt
125g caster sugar
100g maple syrup
1 teaspoon vanilla extract
3 large eggs, lightly beaten
150ml buttermilk,
at room temperature

For the frosting

3 large egg whites
100g caster sugar
1 pinch salt
150g maple syrup
Chocolate-covered toffee candies

Equipment

2 x 20cm diameter cake tins
Baking parchment
Food processor
Electric mixer

1. Pre-heat the oven to 180°C/160°C fan/gas mark 4. Butter the bases of the cake tins and line with buttered baking parchment.

2. Place the pecan nuts on a baking tray and toast lightly on the middle shelf for 5 minutes. Remove from the oven and allow to cool. Pick out the best-looking 12 pecans and set aside. Blitz the remaining pecan nuts in a food processor, until finely chopped.

3. Sift together the flour, baking powder, bicarbonate of soda, cinnamon, nutmeg and salt, and set aside.

4. Mix the butter and caster sugar for about 3 minutes in an electric mixer, until pale and fluffy. Add the maple syrup and vanilla extract and mix for another minute or so. Gradually add the egg, mixing well between each addition.

5. Fold about a third of the sifted ingredients into the mixture, and a third of the buttermilk. Repeat with another third, and again, until everything is folded in. Add the chopped pecan nuts and fold them in too.

6. Divide the mixture between the prepared tins and bake on the middle shelf of the oven for 25 minutes or until golden and risen. Swap the tins around half way through baking to ensure they cook evenly. A wooden skewer should come out clean when you insert it into the middle.

7. Cool the cakes in the tins for 4 minutes, then turn out carefully onto a wire rack to cool properly.

8. For the frosting, put the egg whites, sugar, salt and a tablespoon of water in a heatproof bowl, over a pan of simmering water. The bowl should sit deeply in the pan, half of it below the rim, but the bottom should not touch the water. Pour the maple syrup into another small saucepan over a medium heat, bring to the boil and cook until reduced by half.

9. Meanwhile, whisk the egg white mixture until the sugar has dissolved and it thickens into glossy white 'clouds' or forms peaks.

10. Pour the hot maple syrup into the egg whites, whisking until they are hot, glossy and smooth. Quickly scoop into an electric mixer bowl, and whisk on medium-high for 3 minutes until cool, thick and glossy.

11. Working quickly (the frosting sets as it cools), place one cake on a serving plate and spread with frosting. Cover with the second cake and more frosting, then cover the top and sides of the whole cake using a palette knife to create swirls.

12. Decorate with the pecan nuts you saved and roughly chopped chocolate-covered toffee candies. Leave for an hour for the frosting to set before serving.

Makes 12

30 mins preparation
plus 20 mins chilling
30 mins cooking

Herby Sausage Roll Plaits

Much more than a humble sausage roll, these tasty plaits are perfect at a festive lunch or party.

Ingredients

450g premium sausagemeat
4 large spring onions
2 tablespoons finely
chopped parsley
1 tablespoon finely chopped sage
2 teaspoons dry mustard powder
1 teaspoon cayenne pepper
1 teaspoon garlic granules
Salt and freshly ground
black pepper
Plain flour for rolling out
375g all-butter puff pastry
2 tablespoons milk
1 egg, beaten
1 tablespoon poppy or
sesame seeds

Equipment

Large baking sheet lined with
baking parchment

1. Place the sausagemeat in a mixing bowl. Trim and finely chop the spring onions, and add to the bowl along with the chopped parsley and sage. Add the mustard powder, cayenne pepper and garlic granules, and season well with salt and black pepper. Mix together thoroughly – this is easiest using your hands.

2. On a lightly floured work surface, roll out the pastry into a large rectangle, roughly 40cm x 25cm, keeping the shorter side nearest to you. Trim the edges to neaten and cut the rectangle in half to make two long, thin rectangles, each 40cm x 12cm.

3. Divide the sausagemeat in two. Using damp hands, shape each half into a long, thin sausage, roughly the same thickness as a chipolata and the same length as the pastry. Place the sausagemeat down the middle of each pastry rectangle.

4. Brush the pastry with milk. Cut the pastry on both sides of the sausagemeat into diagonal 1cm wide strips – you will need an even number of strips on each side. Starting at the top right of the first roll, fold one strip up and over the sausage, then fold over the first strip on the left to cover it. Repeat this alternate folding or plaiting all the way down the sausage roll.

5. Repeat with the second roll. Cut each roll into 6 even-sized portions and arrange on the lined baking sheet. Chill in the fridge for 20 minutes while you pre-heat the oven to 180°C/160°C fan/gas mark 4.

6. Mix the egg into any remaining milk and brush over the top of the sausage rolls. Scatter with poppy or sesame seeds.

7. Bake the sausage rolls on the middle shelf of the oven for 30 minutes or until the pastry is crisp and golden brown.

FESTIVE GIFTS

It's the time for giving, and homemade gifts are so much nicer than anything you can buy in the shops. Even better, these are gifts you can eat! I've really enjoyed getting creative with these recipes, and I hope you will too. Of course, how you package them is up to you, but I've given you some ideas to get started with.

Serves 10

30 mins preparation
plus 2 hours chilling
and proving
1 hour cooking

Panettone

Although it originates in Italy, this sweet loaf has become
a Christmas classic here too – with irresistible vanilla and
fruit flavours.

Ingredients

75g raisins
100g candied or mixed peel,
finely chopped
100g glacé cherries
3 tablespoons brandy or dark rum
Finely grated zest of
1 unwaxed lemon
Finely grated zest of 1 orange
450g strong white bread flour,
plus extra for dusting
50g caster sugar
7g fast-action dried yeast
½ teaspoon salt
1 large egg
3 large egg yolks
1 teaspoon vanilla bean paste
150g unsalted butter, softened
100ml whole milk
Pearl sugar for decorating

For the egg wash
1 egg yolk
1 tablespoon milk

Equipment
Electric mixer with dough hook
18cm deep, loose-bottomed
cake tin

1. Tip the raisins and chopped peel into a small pan. Rinse the cherries,
   pat dry, cut into quarters and add to the pan with the brandy or rum.
   Set over a low heat and warm the liquid, but do not let it boil. Remove
   from the heat, add the lemon and orange zest and set aside for
   20 minutes, letting the fruit plump up and infuse.

2. Place the flour in the bowl of an electric mixer with a dough hook.
   Alternatively, if you do not have an electric mixer, use a bowl and mix by
   hand. Add the caster sugar, yeast and salt, and mix well. Make a well in
   the middle and add the whole egg, yolks, vanilla and softened butter.

3. Warm the milk, then pour into the bowl and mix on a low speed for
   about 5 minutes, until the dough is smooth and elastic. Lift the dough
   from the bowl and shape into a neat ball. Return the dough to the bowl,
   cover with cling film. Set aside in a warming drawer or draught-free place
   for about 2 hours, or until the dough has doubled in size.

4. Meanwhile, grease the cake tin with butter and line the base and sides
   with a double layer of buttered baking parchment. The lining around the
   sides should come to about 4cm above the top of the tin.

5. Turn the dough out onto a lightly floured work surface. Add the soaked
   dried fruit and knead until mixed into the dough. It will be quite sticky,
   but resist the temptation to add more flour.

6. Shape the dough into a neat, tight ball and place into the prepared tin,
   seam side down. Cover loosely with oiled cling film. Leave in a warming
   drawer or draught-free place for another 2 hours, or until the dough has
   at least doubled in size again and reached the top of the tin.

7. Pre-heat the oven to 170°C/150°C fan/gas mark 3.

8. Make the egg wash by beating the egg yolk and milk together. Brush it
   gently over the top of the panettone. Scatter with pearl sugar and bake
   in the bottom third of the oven for 20 minutes. Then reduce the heat
   to 150°C/130°C fan/gas mark 2 and continue to cook for another
   35-40 minutes, until the panettone is well risen and golden brown in
   colour, and sounds hollow when you tap it.

9. Leave to cool in the tin for 30 minutes, then transfer to a wire rack.

Chef's note... to remove the loaf simply tap on the bottom of the tin.

20 mins preparation
plus 45 mins cooling time
35 mins cooking

Biscotti Two-Ways

These crisp Italian cookies are perfect with a creamy dessert or after dinner with an espresso or glass of Vin Santo dessert wine. The main recipe here is the traditional one with whole almonds – see the chef's note below for a rich chocolate and pistachio variation.

Ingredients
Traditional Biscotti

100g whole almonds
275g plain flour
150g caster sugar
½ teaspoon baking powder
1 teaspoon anise seeds
1 pinch salt
Finely grated zest of ½ orange
Finely grated zest of ½ lemon
2 large eggs
1 tablespoon Marsala wine or orange juice
1 teaspoon vanilla extract

Chocolate and Pistachio Biscotti

75g pistachios (shelled and unsalted)
230g plain flour
175g caster sugar
40g cocoa
½ teaspoon baking powder
1 pinch salt
1 teaspoon finely grated orange zest
75g dark chocolate, chopped or chips
2 large eggs
1 large egg yolk
1 tablespoon Marsala wine or orange juice
1 teaspoon vanilla extract

Equipment
2 baking sheets lined with baking parchment

1. Pre-heat the oven to 170°C/150°C fan/gas mark 3.

2. Chop the almonds roughly and tip into a large mixing bowl with the plain flour, caster sugar, baking powder, anise seeds and salt. Add the grated orange and lemon zest. Mix thoroughly and make a well in the centre.

3. In a separate bowl, beat together the eggs, Marsala (or orange juice) and vanilla extract. Pour the egg mixture into the well and mix thoroughly until the dough forms a smooth ball. It is best to start by using a wooden spoon or a rubber spatula – then use your hands to make the ball.

4. Dust your hands lightly with plain flour. Divide the dough in two and roll each piece into a log, roughly 20cm long and 5cm in diameter. Arrange the logs on a lined baking sheet, spaced apart so they can spread during baking. Bake on the middle shelf of the oven for 20-25 minutes or until light golden in colour, turning the tray around after 10-15 minutes to ensure the logs brown evenly.

5. Remove from the oven and leave to cool for 45 minutes. Turn the oven down to 150°C/130°C fan/gas mark 2.

6. Using a long serrated knife, cut the cooled biscotti logs on the diagonal into slices about 5mm thick. Lay the slices, spaced apart in a single layer on two lined baking sheets and return to the oven for a further 10 minutes, until they are pale golden brown and crisp. Halfway through the baking time, turn the biscotti over and swap the baking sheets around to ensure they crisp evenly. Cool and keep in an airtight box until you need them, this way they will keep for up to a week.

Chef's note... To make the Chocolate and Pistachio Biscotti, follow the 6 steps above, but use the separate ingredients list, replacing the almonds with pistachios, anise seeds with cocoa, and lemon zest with chopped chocolate. There's also an extra egg yolk.

Cheese Sables

Your homemade gifts do not have to be sweet. These crunchy, crumbly biscuits are wonderfully indulgent.

Ingredients

175g plain flour,
plus extra for dusting
½ teaspoon salt
½ teaspoon cayenne pepper
½ teaspoon dry mustard powder
1 teaspoon cumin or caraway
seeds, lightly crushed
Freshly ground black pepper
150g unsalted butter,
chilled and diced
75g finely grated mature Cheddar
75g finely grated Parmesan
50g sesame seeds
50g kalonji or black sesame seeds
1 tablespoon milk

Equipment

Food processor
Baking sheet lined with
baking parchment

1. Place the flour, salt, cayenne pepper, mustard powder, and cumin or caraway seeds into the bowl of a food processor. Season with black pepper.

2. Add the diced butter and use the pulse button on the food processor to rub it into the dry ingredients. Add the grated cheeses and pulse again until the dough just comes together – you may need to add a drop of water.

3. Tip the dough onto a lightly floured work surface. Roll into a neat, tight log, roughly 5cm in diameter. Wrap in cling film and chill in the fridge for about 2 hours or until really firm.

4. Pre-heat the oven to 180°C/160°C fan/gas mark 4.

5. Tip the sesame and kalonji seeds onto a tray and mix together. Brush the dough log with milk and roll in the seeds to coat evenly. Slice the log into 4-5mm thick discs, and arrange these on the lined baking sheet, spacing them well apart.

6. Bake on the middle shelf of the oven for 12-14 minutes or until crisp and golden.

7. Once completely cold, pack the sables in pretty boxes or cellophane bags.

Makes about 16
20 mins preparation
12 mins cooking

You can vary the fruit and nut combination in these biscuits to suit your tastes – but try to choose bright colours for a more festive look.

Ingredients

75g glacé cherries, preferably natural coloured
75g chopped mixed candied peel
50g blanched almonds
25g shelled and unsalted slivered pistachios
25g flaked almonds
25g unsalted butter
50g demerara sugar
1 tablespoon clear honey
2 tablespoons double cream
25g plain flour
1 pinch ground ginger
1 pinch salt
175g dark chocolate
75g white chocolate

Equipment

2 baking sheets lined with baking parchment
Disposable piping bag

1. Pre-heat the oven to 170°C/150°C fan/gas mark 3.

2. Rinse the glacé cherries to remove any sticky syrup, then pat dry on kitchen paper. Quarter the cherries and place in a bowl with the candied peel. Chop the blanched almonds and add to the cherries along with the slivered pistachios and flaked almonds. Mix to combine and set aside.

3. Melt the butter, demerara sugar and honey in a small pan over a low heat, stirring constantly to prevent the sugar catching on the bottom of the pan. Add the double cream, mix to combine and pour into the bowl of fruit and nuts. Mix well to combine. Add the plain flour, ground ginger and salt, and mix again until smooth.

4. Spoon level dessertspoons of the mixture onto the lined baking sheets, leaving plenty of space between each mound. Flatten them slightly with the back of a spoon. Bake on the middle shelf of the oven for 12 minutes or until the edges of the Florentines are tinged with golden brown.

5. Remove from the oven and leave to cool on the baking sheets until crisp.

6. Melt the dark and white chocolate separately in heatproof glass or ceramic bowls set over pans of barely simmering water, or in the microwave on a low setting. Stir until smooth, remove from the heat and leave to cool slightly. Spread the underside of each Florentine with an even layer of melted dark chocolate. Spoon the melted white chocolate into a disposable piping bag and snip the end into a fine point. Pipe evenly spaced lines of white chocolate over the dark chocolate and drag the point of a wooden skewer or cocktail stick through the lines to make a delicate feathered pattern in the chocolate. Leave until the chocolate has set and hardened before serving.

Chef's note... For the perfect gift, place the Florentines in either pretty cellophane bags or in boxes between layers of waxed or greaseproof paper.

15 mins preparation
plus 1 hour proving
30 mins cooking

Salted Pretzel Sticks with Chocolate Caramel Dipping Sauce

Simple but luxurious, these pretzels always impress. You can dip them in chocolate sauce or lightly drizzle over the top.

Ingredients

Dough
175g plain flour,
plus extra for rolling out
175g strong white flour
4g fast-action dried yeast
a pinch of salt
3 teaspoons soft light brown sugar
225ml warm water

To cook
1 rounded tablespoon bicarbonate
of soda
2 tablespoons soft
light brown sugar
1 egg beaten with 1 tablespoon milk
2-3 teaspoons sea salt flakes or
sesame seeds
2 litre water

Equipment
2-3 parchment lined baking sheets

Chocolate sauce
125g caster sugar
Freshly squeezed juice of 1 orange
150ml double cream
100g dark chocolate, finely chopped
1 teaspoon unsalted butter
a good pinch sea salt flakes
2 tablespoons hot water

1. Tip the flours into a free-standing mixer fitted with a dough hook. Add the yeast, sugar and a pinch of salt. Mix well to combine. Add 225ml warm water and mix on medium speed until thoroughly combined. Continue mixing until the dough is smooth and elastic – this will take about 5 minutes and the dough will be slightly sticky.

2. Shape the dough into a ball, return to the bowl, cover loosely with cling film and leave for 1 hour to rise at room temperature.

3. Preheat the oven to 190°C/170°C fan/gas mark 5.

4. Turn the dough out onto a lightly floured work surface and knead lightly for 20 seconds to knock back any air pockets. Cut the dough into even quarters – it is easier to work the dough in smaller quantities – cut the first quarter into 8 even sized pieces and shape into balls. Using your hands roll each of the dough balls into rough ropes each about 10cm long and set aside for 2 minutes to let the gluten relax slightly. Roll each rope out neatly to a length of about 12cm and no thicker than 1cm. Place on parchment lined baking sheets and set aside, uncovered, while you roll out the remaining dough in the same way.

5. Meanwhile bring 2 litres of water to the boil with the bicarbonate of soda, soft brown sugar and a heaped teaspoon of salt.

6. Gently lower the first batch of 8 pretzel ropes into the simmering water and cook gently for 30 seconds to 1 minute, until they float to the surface and firm up. Remove from the pan with a slotted spoon and drain briefly on kitchen paper before returning to the parchment lined tray. Poach all of the pretzels in the same way.

7. Brush the pretzels with egg wash, sprinkle with salt or sesame seeds and bake for 15 minutes until golden brown and starting to crisp.

8. To make the sauce: Tip the sugar into a small saucepan and add 2 tablespoons hot water. Set the pan over a low heat to dissolve the sugar without stirring. Once all of the sugar has dissolved bring the syrup to the boil and cook steadily until it becomes an amber-coloured caramel. Remove the pan from the heat and carefully add the orange juice – the caramel will hiss and splutter quite dramatically and may well harden in the pan. Return to a low heat to re-melt the hardened caramel, once it is silky smooth add the cream and heat to just below boiling. Remove from the heat, add the chopped chocolate, butter and a good pinch of sea salt flakes and stir until smooth.

Accompaniments

For the perfect partner to any of the savoury dishes in this book, try these tasty recipes. Pickled Cucumber Salad goes perfectly with Rye and Mixed Seed Bread (see page 40) – perhaps with some cold meats – and Mustard Dip is lovely with Carrot and Courgette Loaf (see page 44) or Herby Sausage Roll Plaits (see page 56).

Pickled Cucumber Salad

Ingredients
1 cucumber,
peeled and thinly sliced
1 teaspoon sea salt
1 teaspoon caster sugar
4 tablespoons white wine vinegar
1 tablespoon yellow mustard seeds
Freshly ground black pepper

1. Place the sliced cucumber in a colander and sprinkle with sea salt. Set aside for 1 hour to allow the water to drain from the cucumber.

2. Rinse the sliced cucumber and pat dry with kitchen paper. Place in a bowl, add the sugar, vinegar and mustard seeds, and season with black pepper.

Mustard Dip

Ingredients
250g cream cheese
3 teaspoons grainy mustard
1 teaspoon Dijon mustard
1 tablespoon crème fraîche
or soured cream
1 tablespoon finely snipped chives
Salt and freshly ground black pepper

1. Combine all the ingredients in a mixing bowl and season with salt and black pepper.

Accompaniments

With many of the Christmas treats in this book, it is nice to have something delicious to serve alongside – like Cinnamon Custard with Gingery Plum Pudding (see page 30), Clementine and Brandy Butter with Mincemeat Crumble Pies (see page 48), or a warming mug of Hot Chocolate with one of the festive cakes.

Cinnamon Custard

Ingredients

600ml whole milk
½ vanilla pod or 1 teaspoon vanilla bean paste
1 large cinnamon stick
5 medium egg yolks
50g golden caster sugar
2 tablespoons brandy, optional

1. Pour the milk into a saucepan. Split the vanilla pod in half and add to the pan along with the cinnamon stick. Bring slowly to the boil then remove from the heat and leave to one side for about 30 minutes so the milk becomes infused with the vanilla and cinnamon.

2. In a large bowl, beat the egg yolks and sugar until pale and creamy. Reheat the milk and pour onto the egg mixture, whisking constantly until smooth. Pour the custard back into the pan, place over a low heat and stir constantly until the custard is thick enough to coat the back of a spoon and add the brandy if using – do not let it boil or you might scramble the eggs.

3. Strain into a jug and serve immediately.

Clementine and Brandy Butter

Ingredients

175g unsalted butter, at room temperature
75g icing sugar, sifted
50g soft light brown sugar
¼ teaspoon ground cinnamon
1 good grating of nutmeg
Finely grated zest of 1 clementine
3 tablespoons brandy

1. Beat the soft butter with both sugars until light, creamy and smooth. Add the cinnamon, nutmeg and clementine zest and mix again.

2. Gradually add the brandy, mixing well until thoroughly incorporated. Serve at room temperature.

Hot Chocolate

Ingredients

150g dark chocolate (68%)
50g milk chocolate
350ml semi-skimmed milk
100ml double cream
1 cinnamon stick
2-3 tablespoons maple syrup or clear honey
1 teaspoon vanilla extract
1 pinch salt
Whipped cream and marshmallows to serve

1. Chop both of the chocolates and place in a mixing bowl or jug.

2. In a medium-sized saucepan, combine the milk and cream. Add the cinnamon stick, maple syrup or honey, vanilla extract and salt. Slowly bring to the boil over a low heat to let the cinnamon infuse the milk and cream.

3. Pour the hot milk mixture over the chopped chocolate and whisk until smooth. Return the mixture to the pan and gently reheat, whisking constantly, until just below boiling point. Pour into mugs or heatproof glasses, (depending on the size of these, this recipe is enough for at least two servings). Top with whipped cream and marshmallows and serve immediately.

About Howdens Joinery

Howdens Joinery offers a range of integrated kitchens, appliances and joinery products designed to meet the needs of modern living.

Our offer includes over 50 different kitchen designs, plus a full range of accessories, worktops, doors, flooring, skirting, and a wide variety of Lamona appliances, sinks and taps, exclusive to Howdens. The Lamona range has been selected to perfectly complement our range of kitchens and products are manufactured to the highest standards to ensure they are durable and reliable. Last year we supplied over 400,000 kitchens, 750,000 appliances and 650,000 sinks and taps to UK homes.

With a fine balance of minimal design and ample storage, this kitchen is perfect for both everyday use and family celebrations, such as Christmas. The contrast of modern, light gloss colours with natural finishes creates a spacious yet homely feel. Plus, the bespoke shelving and hidden cubby-holes are the perfect addition, providing practical storage for necessities – and a Christmas decoration or two!

To find out more or contact one of over 630 nationwide depots, visit **www.howdens.com**

Bespoke shelving

Full-height pull & swing larder and bespoke shelving

Lamona Belmont 1.5 bowl sink with Lamona Chrome Enza monobloc tap

Lamona touch control integrated combination microwave,
Lamona warming drawer and Lamona touch control single pyrolytic oven

Oak Block and White Glass Effect worktops

About the author

Bestselling author, freelance food stylist and recipe writer Annie Rigg has written many books on baking and confectionery – including popular titles such as Decorating Cakes and Cookies, Make, Bake and Celebrate! and Gifts from the Kitchen. She also contributes features to food and lifestyle magazines, including Sainsbury's Magazine, Waitrose Kitchen, Delicious, Olive, Jamie Magazine, and Red.

As a food stylist, Annie works for leading cookbook publishers and photographers – and with some of our best-known chefs and writers, such as Mary Berry, Phil Vickery, Rachel Allen, Martha Collison and Xanthe Clay.

Annie lives in both London and Hampshire with her faithful Jack Russell, Mungo, always by her side.